H.G. WELLS

H.G. WELLS

J.D. BERESFORD

WILDSIDE PRESS

H.G. WELLS

CONTENTS

I

INTRODUCTION:
THE NORMALITY OF MR WELLS

In his Preface to the *Unpleasant Plays*, Mr Shaw boasts his possession of "normal sight." The adjective is the oculist's, and the application of it is Mr Shaw's, but while the phrase is misleading until it is explained to suit a particular purpose, it has a pleasing adaptability, and I can find none better as a key to the works of Mr H.G. Wells.

We need not bungle over the word "normal," in any attempt to meet the academic objection that it implies conformity to type. In this connection, the gifted possessor of normal sight is differentiated from his million neighbours by the fact that he wears no glasses; and if a few happy people still exist here and there who have no need for the mere physical assistance, the number of those whose mental outlook is undistorted by tradition, prejudice or some form of bias is so small that we regard them as inspired or criminal according to the inclination of our own beloved predilection. And no spectacles will correct the mental astigmatism of the multitude, a fact that is often a cause of considerable annoyance to the possessors of normal sight. That defect of vision, whether congenital or induced by the confinements of early training, persists and increases throughout life, like other forms of myopia. The man who sees a ball as slightly flattened, like a tangerine orange too tightly packed (an "oblate spheroid" would be the physicist's brief description), seeks the society of other men who share his illusion; and the company of them take arms against the opposing faction, which is confirmed in the belief that the ball is egg-shaped, that the bulge, in fact, is not "oblate" but "prolate."

I will not elaborate the parable; it is sufficient to indicate that in my reading of Mr Wells, I have seen him as regarding all life from a reasonable distance. By good fortune he avoided the influences of his early training, which was too ineffectual to leave any permanent mark upon him. His readers may infer, from certain descriptions in *Kipps*, and *The History of Mr Polly*, that Wells himself sincerely regrets the inadequacies of that "private school of dingy aspect and still dingier pretensions, where there were no object lessons, and the studies of book-keeping and French were pursued (but never effectually overtaken) under the guidance of an elderly gentleman, who wore a nondescript gown and took snuff, wrote copperplate, explained nothing, and used a cane with remarkable dexterity and gusto." But, properly considered, that inadequate elderly gentleman may be regarded as our benefactor. If he had been more apt in his methods, he might have influenced the blessed normality of his pupil, and bound upon him the spectacles of his own order. Worse still, Mr Wells might have been born into the leisured classes, and sent to Eton and Christchurch, and if his genius had found any expression after that awful experience, he would probably, at the best, have written polite essays or a history of Napoleon, during the intervals of his leisured activity as a member of the Upper House.

Happily, Fate provided a scheme for preserving his eyesight, and pitched him into the care of Mr and Mrs Joseph Wells on the 21st September 1866; behind or above a small general shop in Bromley. Mrs Wells was the daughter of an innkeeper at Midhurst and had been in service as a lady's maid before her marriage. Joseph Wells had had a more distinguished career. He had been a great Kent bowler in the early sixties, and it must have been, I think, only the year before the subject of our essay appeared at Bromley that his father took four wickets with consecutive balls and created a new record in the annals of cricket. The late Sir Francis Galton might have made something out of this ancestry; I must confess that it is entirely beyond my powers, although I make the reservation that we know little of the abilities of H.G. Wells' mother. She has not figured as a recognisable portrait in any of his novels.

The Bromley shop, like most of its kind, was a failure. Moderate success might have meant a Grammar School for young Wells, and the temptations of property, but Fate gave our young radical another twist by thrusting him temporarily within sight of an alien and magnificent prosperity, where as the son of the housekeeper at Up Park, near Petersfield, he might recognise his immense separation from the members of the ruling class, as described in *Tono-Bungay*.

After that came "the drapery," first at Windsor and then at Southsea; but we have no autobiography of this period, only the details of the trade and its circumstances. For neither Hoopdriver, nor Kipps, nor Polly could have qualified for the post of assistant at Midhurst Grammar School, a position that H.G. Wells obtained at sixteen after he had broken his indentures with the Southsea draper.

At this point we come up with Mr Lewisham, and may follow him in his experiences after he obtained what was, in fact, a scholarship at the Normal School of Science, South Kensington; but we drop that hero again before his premature marriage and failure, to follow the uncharted course of Wells obtaining his B.Sc. with first-class honours; passing to an assistant-mastership at the Henley House School, St

John's Wood, and so coming by way of tutor, lecturer and demonstrator to the beginnings of journalism, to the breaking of a blood-vessel and thence, without further diversion, to the trade of letters, somewhere in the summer of 1893.

I lave taken as my text the normality of Mr Wells, on the understanding that I shall define the essential term as I will; and this brief outline of his early experiences may help to show, *inter alia*, that he viewed life from many angles before he was twenty-seven. That he had the capacity so to see life was either a lucky accident or due to some untraceable composition of heredity. That he kept his power was an effect of his casual education. He was fortunate enough to escape training in his observation of the sphere.

Persistent repetition will finally influence the young mind, however gifted, and if Mr Wells had been subject to the discipline of what may be called an efficient education, he might have seen his sphere at the age of twenty-seven as slightly flattened — whether it appeared oblate or prolate is no consequence — and I could not have crowned him with the designation that heads this Introduction.

He is, in fact, normal just in so far as his gift of vision was undistorted by the precepts and dogmas of his parents, teachers and early companions.

II

THE ROMANCES

Mr Wells' romances have little or nothing in common with those of Jules Verne, not even that peculiar quality of romance which revels in the impossible. The heroes of Jules Verne were idealised creatures making use of some wonderful invention for their own purposes; and the future of mankind was of no account in the balance against the lust for adventure under new mechanical conditions. Also, Jules Verne's imagination was at the same time mathematical and Latin; and he was entirely uninfluenced by the writings of Comte.

Mr Wells' experiments with the relatively improbable have become increasingly involved with the social problem, and it would be possible to trace the growth of his opinions from this evidence alone, even if we had not the valuable commentary afforded by his novels and his essays in sociology. But his interest in the present and future welfare of man would not in the first place have prompted him to the writing of romance (unless it had been cast in the severely allegorical form of *The Pilgrim's Progress*), and if we are to account for that ebullition, we shall be driven — like Darwin with his confounding peacock — to take refuge in some theory of exuberance. The later works have been so defensive and, in one sense, didactic that one is apt to forget that many of the earlier books, and all the short stories, must have originated in the effervescence of creative imagination.

Mr Wells must, also, have been slightly intoxicated by

the first effects of reaction. A passage from *The Future in America* exhibits him somewhat gleefully reviving thoughts of the prison-house, and I quote it in order to account for his first exercises in prophecy by a study of contrasts. "I remember," he writes, "that to me in my boyhood speculation about the Future was a monstrous joke. Like most people of my generation, I was launched into life with millennial assumptions. This present sort of thing, I believed, was going on for a time, interesting personally, perhaps, but as a whole inconsecutive, and then — it might be in my lifetime or a little after it — there would be trumpets and shoutings and celestial phenomena, a battle of Armageddon, and the Judgment. . . . To talk about the Man of the year Million was, of course, in the face of this great conviction, a whimsical play of fancy. The year Million was just as impossible, just as gaily nonsensical as fairyland. . . ."

The imprisoning bottle was opened when he became a student of biology, under Huxley, and the liquid of his suppressed thought began to bubble. He prefaced his romances by a sketch in the old *Pall Mall Gazette*, entitled *The Man of the Year Million*, an a priori study that made one thankful for one's prematurity. After that physiological piece of logic, however, he tried another essay in evolution, published in 1895 in book form under the title of *The Time Machine* — the first of his romances.

The machine itself is the vaguest of mechanical assumptions; a thing of ivory, quartz, nickel and brass that quite illogically carries its rider into an existing past or future. We accept the machine as a literary device to give an air of probability to the essential thing, the experience; and forget the means in the effect. The criterion of the prophecy in this case is influenced by the theory of "natural selection." Mr Wells' vision of the "Sunset of Mankind" was of men so nearly adapted to their environment that the need for struggle, with its corollary of the extermination of the unfit, had practically ceased. Humanity had become differentiated into two races, both recessive; one, the Eloi, a race of child-like, simple, delicate creatures living on the surface of a kindly earth; the other, the Morlocks, a more active but debased race, of bestial habits, who lived underground and preyed cannibalistically on the surface-dwellers whom they helped to preserve, as a man may preserve game. The Eloi, according to the hypothesis of the Time Traveller, are the descendants of the leisured classes; the Morlocks of the workers. "The Eloi, like the Carlovingian kings, had decayed to a mere beautiful futility. They still possessed the earth on sufferance; since the Morlocks, subterranean for innumerable generations, had come at last to find the day-lit surface intolerable. And the Morlocks made their garments, I inferred, and maintained them in their habitual needs perhaps through the survival of an old habit of service." All this is in the year 802,701 A.D.

The prophecy is less convincing than the wonderful sight of the declining earth some million years later, sinking slowly into the dying fires of the worn-out sun. Man and the vertebrates have disappeared, and the highest wonder of animal life is represented by giant crustaceans, which in turn give way to a lower form. We have a vision of an involution that shall succeed the highest curve of development; of life ending where it began in the depths of the sea, as the initial energy of the solar system is dissipated and the material of it returns to rest at the temperature of the absolute zero. And the picture is made more horrible to the imaginative by the wonder whether the summit of the evolutionary curve has not already been reached — or it may be passed in the days of the Greek philosophers.

The Time Machine, despite certain obvious faults of imagination and style, is a brilliant fantasy; and it affords a valuable picture of the young Wells looking at the world, with his normal eyes, and finding it, more particularly, incomplete. At the age of twenty-seven or so, he has freed himself very completely from the bonds of conventional thought, and is prepared to examine, and to present life from the detached standpoint of one who views it all from a respectable distance; but who is able, nevertheless — an essential qualification — to enter life with all the passion and generosity of his own humanity.

And in *The Wonderful Visit* — published in the same year as *The Time Machine* — he comes closer to earth. That ardent ornithologist, the Rev. K. Hilyer, Vicar of Siddermouth, who brought down an angel with a shot-gun, is tenderly imagined; a man of gentle mind, for all the limitations of his training. The mortalised angel, on the other hand, is rather a tentative and simple creature. He may represent, perhaps, the rather blank mind of one who sees country society without having had the inestimable privilege of learning how it came about. His temperament was something too childlike — without the child's brutality — to investigate the enormous complexities of adjustment that had brought about the conditions into which he was all too suddenly plunged by a charge of duck-shot. He came and was filled with an inalterable perplexity, but some of his questions were too ingenuous; and while we may sympathise with the awful inertia of Hilyer before the impossible task of explaining the inexplicable differences between mortal precept and mortal practice, we feel that we might, in some cases at least, have made a more determined effort. We might have found some justification for chairs, by way of instance, and certainly an excuse for raising beds above the floor. But the wounded angel, like the metal machine, is only a device whereby the searching examination of our author may be displayed in an engrossing and intimate form. And in *The Wonderful Visit*, that exuberance we postulated, that absorption in the development of idea, is more marked; in the unfolding of the story we can trace the method of the novelist.

Indeed, the three romances that follow discover hardly a trace of the social investigator. *The Island of Dr Moreau, The Invisible Man* and *The War of the Worlds* are essays in pure fantasy, and although the first of the three is influenced by biology I class it unhesitatingly among the works of sheer exuberance. Each of these books is, in effect, an answer to some rather whimsical question, and the problem that Dr Moreau attempted to solve was: "Can we, by surgery, so accelerate the evolutionary process as to make man out of a beast in a few days or weeks?" And within limits he found that the answer was: "Yes."

In the seclusion of his island, and with the poor assistance of the outlawed medical student, Montgomery, Dr Moreau succeeded in producing some creditable parodies of humanity by his operations on pigs, bulls, dogs and other animals. These cut and remoulded creatures had something the appearance and intelligence of Homo Sapiens, and could be maintained at that level by the exercise of discipline and the constant recital of "the Law"; left to themselves they gradually reverted to the habits and manners of the individual beasts out of which they had been carved. We may infer that some subtle organic chemistry worked its determination upon their uncontrolled wills, but Mr Wells offers no explanation, psychic, chemical or biological, and I do not think that he intended any particular fable beyond the evident one that, physically, one species is as like to the next as makes no matter. What Moreau did well another man might have done better. It is a good story, and the adventures of the marooned Prendick, alone, are sufficient justification for the original conception. (I feel bound to note, however, the absurd comments of some early reviewers who seemed to imagine that the story was a defence of vivisection.)

The next romance (1897) seeks to answer the question: "What could a man do if he were invisible?" Various attempts to answer that question had been made by other writers, but none of them had come to it with Mr Wells' practical grasp of the real problem; the earlier romantics had not grappled with the necessity for clothes and the various ways in which a material man, however indistinguishable his body by our sense of sight, must leave traces of his passage. The study from beginning to end is finely realistic; and even the theory of the albino, Griffin, and in a lesser degree his method of winning the useless gift of invisibility, are convincing enough to make us wonder whether the thing is not scientifically possible. As a pure romance set in perfectly natural surroundings, *The Invisible Man* is possibly the highwater mark of Mr Wells' achievement in this kind. He has perfected his technique, and the interest in the development of the story works up steadily to the splendid climax, when the form of the berserker Griffin returns to visibility, his hands clenched, his eyes wide open, and on his face an expression of "anger and dismay," the elements – as I choose to think – of man's revolt against imprisonment in the flesh. It is worth while to note that by another statement, the same problem is posed and solved in the short story called *The Country of the Blind*.

The War of the Worlds (1898), although written in the first person, is in some ways the most detached of all these fantasies; and it is in this book that Mr Wells frankly confesses his own occasional sense of separation. "At times," says the narrator of the history, "I suffer from the strangest sense of detachment from myself and the world about me, I seem to watch it all from the outside, from somewhere inconceivably remote, out of time, out of space, out of the stress and tragedy of it all." That sense must have remained with him as he wrote the account of the invading Martians, so little passion does the book contain. The vision, however, is clear enough and there is more invention than in many of the other romances. The picture of the Martians themselves develops in one direction the theory of human evolution expressed in *The Man of the Year Million*. The expansion of the brain case, and the apotheosis of pure intellect, devoid, so far as we can judge, of any emotional expression, are the steadily biological deductions that we should expect from the Wells of this period. The fighting machines of these incomprehensible entities, the heat ray and the black smoke, are all excellent conceptions; and the narrative is splendidly graphic. But only in the scenes with the curate, when the narrator is stirred to passionate anger, and in his later passages with the sapper, do we catch any glimpses of the novelist intrigued with the intimate affairs of humanity. Even the narrator's brother, in his account of the escape with two women in a pony-carriage, has become infected with that sense of detachment. The two women are strongly differentiated but leave little impression of personality.

The fact that I have made this comment on lack of passion in describing one of these earlier romances is indicative of a particular difference between Mr Wells' method in this sort and the method of the lesser writer of fantasias. The latter, whatever his idea, and it may be a brilliant idea, is always intent on elaborating the wonder of his theme by direct description. Mr Wells is far more subtle and more effective. He takes an average individual, identifies him with the world as we know it, and then proceeds gradually to bring his marvel within the range of this individual's apprehension. We see the improbable, not too definitely, through the eyes of one who is prepared with the same incredulity as the reader of the story, and as a result the strange phenomenon, whether fallen angel, invisible man, converted beast or invading Martian, takes all the shape of reality. That this shape is convincing is due to the brilliance of Mr Wells' imagination and his power of graphic expression; the lesser writer might adopt the method and fail utterly to attain the effect; but it is this conception of the means to reach the intelligence and senses of the average reader that chiefly distinguishes these romances from those of such writers as Jules Verne. Our approach to the wonderful is so gradual and so natural that when we are finally confronted with it the incredible thing has become inevitable and expected. Finally, it has become so identified with human surprise, anger or dismay that any failure of humanity in the chief person of the story reacts upon our conception of the wonderful intrusion among familiar phenomena.

Now, this power of creating the semblance of fact out of an ideal was too valuable a thing to be wasted on the making of stories that had no purpose beyond that of interesting or exciting the reader with such imaginations as the Martians, whose only use was to threaten humanity with extinction. Mr Wells' own sight of our blindness, our complacent acceptance of the sphere as an oblate or prolate spheroid, might be, he hoped, another of the marvels which we should come to accept through the medium of romance. So he began tentatively at first to introduce a vivid criticism of the futility of present-day society into his fantasies, and the first and the least of these books was that published in 1899 as *When the Sleeper Wakes*, a title afterwards changed to *The Sleeper Awakes*.

In the two opening chapters we find the same delightfully realistic treatment of the unprecedented slowly mingling with the commonplace. The first appearance of Graham the Sleeper, tormented then by the spectres and doubts that accompany insomnia, is made so credible that we accept his symptoms without the least demur; his condition is merely unusual enough to excite a trembling interest. Even the passing of his early years of trance does not arouse scepticism. But then we fall with one terrific plunge into the world of A.D. 2100, and, like Graham, we cannot realise it. Moreover this changed, developed world has a slightly mechanical air. The immense enclosed London, imagined by Mr Wells, is no Utopia, yet, like the dream of earlier prophets, it is too logical to entice us into any hallucination; and we come, fatally, to a criticism of the syllogism.

Mr Wells himself has confessed, in a new Preface, that this is "one of the most ambitious and least satisfactory" of his books; and explains that it was written against time, when he was on the verge of a serious illness. It is superfluous, therefore, to criticise it in detail, but one or two points in relation to the sociological idea must be emphasised.

The main theme is the growing division between Capital and Labour. The Giant Trust — managing the funds accumulated in Graham's name, a trust that has obtained possession of so immense a capital that it controls the chief activities of the world — is figured in the command of a certain Ostrog, who, with all the dependents that profit by the use of his wealth and such mercenaries as he can hold to himself, represents one party in opposition to the actual workers and producers, generically the People. The picture is the struggle of our own day in more acute form; the result, in the amended edition, is left open. "Who will win — Ostrog or the People?" Mr Wells writes in the Preface referred to above, and answers: "A thousand years hence that will still be just the open question we leave today."

I am not concerned in this place to question the validity of that answer, nor to suggest that the Wells of 1914 would not necessarily give the same account of his beliefs as the Wells of 1909, but I must draw attention to the attitude displayed in the book under consideration in order to point the change of feeling recognisable in later books. In *The Sleeper Awakes*, even in the revised version, the sociological theory is still mechanical, the prophecy at once too logical, and at the same time deduced from premises altogether too restricted. The world of A.D. 2100 is the world of today, with its more glaring contrasts still more glaringly emphasised; with its social incongruities and blindness raised to a higher power. And all that it lacked has been put into a romance called *In the Days of the Comet* (1906), a book to which I shall now leap, returning later to consider the comparatively irrelevant theses of three other romances that chronologically intervened.

The great change wrought by the coming of the Comet might be sentimentally described as a change of heart; I prefer to call it a change of reason. All the earlier part of the work, which is again told in the first person, presents the life of a Midland industrial area as seen by one who has suffered it. The Capital-Labour problem bulks in the foreground, and is adequately supported by a passionate exposition of the narrowness and misery of lower-middle-class life in the jumble of limitations, barriers and injustices that arise from the absolute ownership of property. Also, into this romance – the only one, by the way – comes some examination of the relations of the sexes. And all this jumble is due, if we are to believe the remedy, to human misunderstanding. The influence of the Comet passed over the earth, and men, after a few hours of trance, awoke to a new realisation. We come to a first knowledge of the change in one of the most beautiful passages that Mr Wells has written; and although I dislike to spoil a passage by setting it out unclothed by the idea and expectations which have led to its expression, given it form, and fitted it to a just place in the whole composition, I will make an exception in this case in order to justify my metaphor of "normal sight." The supposed writer of the description had just awakened from the trance induced by the passing of the Comet. He says:

> "I came slowly, stepping very carefully because of those drugged, feebly awakening things, through the barley to the hedge. It was a very glorious hedge, so that it held my eyes. It flowed along and interlaced like splendid music. It was rich with lupin, honeysuckle, campions and ragged robin; bed straw, hops and wild clematis twined and hung among its branches, and all along its ditch border the starry stitchwort lifted its childish faces and chorused in lines and masses. Never had I seen such a symphony of note-like flowers and tendrils and leaves. And suddenly, in its depths, I heard a chirrup and the whir of startled wings.
> "Nothing was dead, but everything had changed to beauty! And I stood for a time with clean and happy eyes looking at the intricate delicacy before me and marvelling how richly God has made his worlds. . . ."

And not only the writer but also every other person on the earth had been miraculously cured of their myopia and astigmatism. They saw beauty and the means to still more perfect beauty, and, seeing, they had but to believe and the old miseries vanished. In the old days men preached a furious denial of self that led to the fatuity of an asceticism such as that of St Simon Stylites. The lesson – I cannot deny that the book is didactic – of the change wrought by the comet is that man should find the full expression of his personality in sympathy and understanding. The egotism remains, but it works to a collective end. . . .

War is necessarily touched upon in this book as an inevitable corollary to the problems of personal and a fortiori of national property; but the real counterblast against wholesale fratricide was reserved for the following romance, published in 1908.

The War in the Air definitely disclosed a change of method that was adumbrated in its predecessor. The agent of experience is still retained in the person of Bert Smallways, but the restrictions imposed by the report of an eyewitness have become too limiting, and, like Hardy in *The Dynasts*, Mr Wells alternates between a near and a distant vision. The Welt-Politik could not be explained through the intelligence of a "little Cockney cad," even though he was "by no means a stupid person and up to a certain limit not badly educated"; and the general development of the world-war, the account of the collapse of the credit system and all such large and general effects necessitated the broad treatment of the historian. So the intimate, personal narrative of Smallways' adventures is occasionally dropped for a few pages; Mr Wells shuts off his magic-lantern and fills the interval with an analysis of larger issues.

And the issues are so vital, the *dénouement* so increasingly probable, that, despite all the exaggerations necessary in a fiction of this kind, the warning contained in this account of a world-war is one that must remain in the minds of any thoughtful reader. Smallways' pert reflection on the causes of the immense downfall represents the wisdom that comes of bitter experience, and the application of it is very pertinent to present conditions. "There was us in Europe all at sixes and sevens with our silly flags and our silly newspapers raggin' us up against each other and keepin' us apart," says Smallways, and for the briefest analysis of causes that continually threaten us with all the useless horrors of war, the summary could scarcely be bettered.

Indeed, I think that *The War in the Air* is the greatest of Mr Wells' achievements in fantasy that has a deeper purpose than mere amusement. The story is absorbing and Smallways a perfectly conceived character, recommendations that serve to popularise the book as a romance; but all the art of the construction is relevant to the theme, and to the logical issue which is faced unflinchingly. In the many wild prophecies that have been incorporated in various stories of a great European war, there has been discoverable now and again some hint of insight into the real dangers that await mankind. But such stories as these degenerate into some accidental, but inferentially glorious, victory of British arms, and any value in the earlier comments is swamped in the sentimentality of the fortuitous, and designedly popular, sequel. In the book now under consideration the conception is too wide for any such lapses into the maudlin. British interests play an insignificant part in the drama. We have to consider war not as an incident in the history of a nation, but as a horrible disgrace in the history of humanity.

And war is the theme also of *The World Set Free* (1914), but it leads here to a theory of reconstruction of which we have no sight in the earlier work. The opening chapters describe the inception of the means, the discovery of the new source of energy — a perfectly reasonable conception —

that led to the invention of the "atomic bomb," a thing so terribly powerful and continuous in its action that after the first free use of it in a European outbreak, war became impossible. As a romance, the book fails. The interest is not centred in a single character, and we are given somewhat disconnected glimpses of various phases in the discovery of the new energy, in its application, and of the catastrophes that follow its use as an instrument of destruction. The essay form has almost dominated the method of the novelist, and consequently the essential parable has not the same force as in *The War in the Air*. Nevertheless, the vision is there, obscured by reason of its more personal expression; and before I return to consider the three less pertinent romances interposed between those that have a more recognisable critical tendency, I wish to sum up the distinctive attitude of the four just considered.

And in this thing I claim that the conscious purpose of the artist is of comparatively small account. I may be doing Mr Wells an injustice, either by robbing him of the credit of a clearly conceived intention, or by reading into his books a deliberation which he might wish to disclaim. But my business is not justice to the author in this sense, but an interpretation − necessarily personal − of the message his books have conveyed to a particular reader. And the plain message that all these romances − including those that follow − have conveyed to me is the necessity for ridding the mind of traditions of the hypnotic suggestions of parents and early teachers, of the parochial influences of immediate surroundings, of the prejudices and self-interested dogmatisms and hyperboles of common literature, especially of the daily and weekly press; in order that we may, if only for an exercise in simple reason, dissociate ourselves for a moment from all those intimate forces, and regard life with the calmness of one detached from personal interests and desires. No human being who has not thus stood apart from life can claim to have realised himself; and in so far as he is unable thus to separate himself temporarily from his circumstances he confesses that he is less a personality than a bundle of reactions to familiar stimuli. But given that power of detachment, the reader may find in these four books matter for the reconsideration of the whole social problem. Whether he accept such tentative reconstructions as those suggested in *The World Set Free* or *In the Days of the Comet* is relatively unimportant, the essential thing is that he should view life with momentarily undistracted eyes; and see both the failures of our civilisation and its potentialities for a finer and more gracious existence. . . .

The First Men in the Moon (1901) is little more than a piece of sheer exuberance. The theory of the means to the adventure and the experience itself are both plausible. There are a few minor discrepancies, but when the chief assumption is granted the deductions will all stand examination. The invention of cavorite, the substance that is impervious to the force — whatever it may be — of gravitation, as other substances are impervious to light, heat, sound or electricity, is not a priori impossible, nor is the theory that the moon is hollow, that the "Selenites" live below the surface, or that evolution has produced on our satellite an intelligent form which, anatomically, is more nearly allied to the insect than to the vertebrate type as we know it. The exposition of lunar social conditions cannot be taken very seriously. Specialisation is the key-note; the production by education and training, of minds, and, as far as possible, bodies, adapted to a particular end, and incapable of performing other technical functions. The picture of this highly developed state, however, is not such as would tempt us to emulation. As a machine it works; as an ideal it lacks any presentation of the thing we call beauty. The apotheosis of intelligence in the concrete example leaves us unambitious in that direction.

One chapter, however, stands apart and elaborates once more that detachment for space and time which I have so particularly emphasised as the more important feature of these particular books. Mr Bedford, alone in his Cavorite sphere between the Earth and the Moon, experiences this sensation of aloofness. "I became, if I may go express it, dissociate from Bedford," he writes. "I looked down on Bedford as a trivial, incidental thing with which I chanced to be connected," Bedford, unfortunately for my moral, was a poor creature who got no benefit from his privilege, who flouted it indeed and regretted his inability "to recover the full-bodied self-satisfaction of his early days." Possibly the fact that in his case the knowledge was thrust upon him may account for his failure. It is only the knowledge we seek that has any influence upon us.

The Sea Lady (1902) stands alone among Mr Wells' romances. The realistic method remains, but the conception is touched with a poetic fancy of a kind that I have not found elsewhere in these books. The Venus Annodomini who came out of the sea at Folkestone in the form of an authentic mermaid was something more than a mere critic of our civilised conventions. She was that, too; she asked why people walked on the Leas "with little to talk about and nothing to look at, and bound not to do all sorts of natural things, and bound to do all sorts of preposterous things." But she was also the personification of "other dreams." She had "the quality of the open sky, of deep tangled places, of the flight of birds . . . of the high sea." She represented to one man, at least, "the Great Outside." And, if we still find a repetition of the old statement in that last description, it is, nevertheless, surrounded with a glamour that is not revealed in such books as *In the Days of the Comet*. The ideal that is faintly shadowed in *The Sea Lady* is more ethereal, less practical; the story, despite the naturalistic, half-cynical manner of its recountal, has the elements of romance. The closing scene describes the perplexity of a practical Kentish policeman "who in the small hours before dawn came upon the wrap the Sea Lady had been wearing, just as the tide overtook it," He stands there on the foreshore with a foolish bewilderment, wondering chiefly "what people are up to." He is the "simple citizen of a plain and obvious world." And Mr Wells concludes: "I picture the interrogation of his lantern going out for a little way, a stain of faint pink curiosity upon the mysterious vast serenity of the night." And I make an application of the parable for my own purposes, and wonder how far the curiosity of Mr Wells' readers will carry them into the great mystery that lies behind the illusion of this apparently obvious world.

We come, finally, without any suggestion of climax, to *The Food of the Gods* (1904). The food was produced, casually in the first instance, by two experimenters who served no cause but that of their own inquisitive science. One of them, Redwood, had become intrigued by the fact that the growth of all living things proceeded with bursts and intermissions; it was as if they had "to accumulate force to grow, grew with vigour only for a time, and then had to wait for a space before they could go on growing again." And Bensington, the other experimenter, succeeded in separating a food that produced regular instead of intermittent growth. It was universal in its effects, influencing vegetable as well as animal life; and in the course of twenty years it produced human giants, forty feet high. This is a theme for Mr Wells to revel in, and he does, treating the detail of the first two-thirds of the book with a fine realism. Like Bensington, he saw, "behind the grotesque shapes and accidents of the present, the coming world of giants and all the mighty things the future has in store – vague and splendid, like some glittering palace seen suddenly in the passing of a sunbeam far away." The parable is plain enough, but the application of it weakens when we realise that so far as the merely physical development goes, the food of the gods is only bringing about a change of scale. If we grant that this "insurgent bigness" must conquer the world, the final result is only humanity in the same relation to life that it now occupies, and we are left to reflect with Bensington, after the vision had faded, on "sinister shadows, vast declivities and darknesses, inhospitable immensities, cold, wild and terrible things."

The change of scale, however, so long as it was changing, presents in another metaphor the old contrasts. The young giants, the Cossars and Redwood, looking down on common humanity from a vantage-point some thirty to forty feet higher than the "little people," are critical by force of circumstances; and they are at the same time handicapped by an inability to comprehend the thing criticised. They are too differentiated; and for the purpose of the fable none of them is gifted with the power to study these insects with the sympathy of a Henri Fabre. We may find some quality of blundering stupidity in the Cossars and in young Redwood, they were too prejudiced by their physical scale; but the simple Caddles, born of peasant parents, uneducated and set to work in a chalk quarry, is the true enquirer. He walked up to London to solve his problem, and his fundamental question: "What's it all *for?*" remained unanswered. The "little people" could not exchange ideas with him, and he never met his brother giants. It is, however, exceedingly doubtful whether they could have offered him any satisfactory explanation of the purpose of the universe. Their only ambition seemed to be reconstruction on a larger scale.

I think the partial failure of *The Food of the Gods* to furnish any ethical satisfaction is due to the fact that in this romance Mr Wells has identified himself too closely with the giants; a fault that indicates a slight departure from normality. The inevitable contrast between great and little lacks a sympathy and appreciation we find elsewhere. "Endless conflict. Endless misunderstanding. All life is that. Great and little cannot understand one another" is the true text of the book; and it implies a weakness in the great not less than in the little; a weakness that is hardly exonerated by the closing sentence: "But in every child born of man lurks some seed of greatness – waiting for the food." I find a quality of reasonableness in the little people's antagonism to the blundering superiority of those giants.

To the tail of these romances I may pin the majority of Mr Wells' short stories. The best of them are all included in the collection published under the title of *The Country of the Blind*. In this form Mr Wells displays nothing but the exuberance of his invention. In the Preface to the collection he defines his conception of short-story writing as "the jolly art of making something very bright and moving; it may be horrible or pathetic or funny, or beautiful, or profoundly illuminating, having only this essential, that it should take from fifteen to twenty minutes to read aloud." I can add nothing to that description, and would only take away from it so much as is implied by the statement that I cannot call to mind any one of these stories which is "profoundly illuminating" in the same sense that I would certainly apply the phrase to some of the romances. Jolly and bright they undoubtedly are, but when they are moving, they provide food for wonder rather than for enlightenment. . . .

I cannot leave these romances without a comment on Mr Wells' justification as preacher and prophet. Writing in the midst of the turmoil of war, I am vividly conscious of having had my mind prepared for it by the material I have here so inadequately described. All the misunderstandings, the weaknesses, the noisy, meaningless ambitions, the tepid acceptance of traditional standards, have been exposed by Mr Wells in these fantasies of his. And in *The War in the Air*, with just such exaggerations as are necessary for a fiction of this kind, he has forecast the conditions which have now overtaken us. We know — or we might know if we had the capacity for any sort of consequent consideration of our conditions — that in a reasonably conducted civilisation no such awful catastrophe as this senseless conflagration could have been possible. No doubt we shall profit by the lesson, but it is one that any individual might have learned for himself from these romances, without paying the fearful price that is now necessary. And because humanity is apt to forget its most drastic punishments, to revert to its original inertia as soon as the smart is healed, I feel that when the worst is over, these books will have a greater value than ever before. I believe that in them may be found just those essentials of detachment and broad vision which might serve to promote a higher and more stable civilisation.

III

THE NOVELS

I am willing to maintain that H.G. Wells is second to none as a writer of romances of the type I have just examined. I am less certain of his position as a novelist. He brings to his fiction the open-eyed recognition of realities, the fine analysis of modern conditions, the lucid consequent thought and the clean, graphic style that mark the qualities of his other method; he has that "poetic gift, the gift of the creative and illuminating phrase," which, he has said, "alone justifies writing"; but he has not the power of creating characters that stand for some essential type of humanity. On the one hand he is inclined to idealise the engineer and the scientific researcher, on the other to satirise and, in effect, to group into one sloppy-thinking mass every other kind of Englishman, not excepting philosophers, politicians and social reformers. This broad generalisation omits any consideration of the merely uneducated, such as Hoopdriver or Kipps, and the many women he has drawn. But the former, however sympathetically treated, are certainly not idealised; and among the latter, the only real creation, in my opinion, is Susan Ponderevo in *Tono-Bungay*; although there is a possible composite of various women in the later books that may represent the general insurgent character of recent young womanhood. But now that I have made this too definite statement I want to go back over it, touch it up and smooth it out. For if I have found Mr Wells' character types too few and too specialised; and as if, with regard to his more or less idealised males — such as Capes, George Ponderevo, Remington, Trafford, Stafford — he had modelled and re-modelled them in the effort to build up one finally estimable figure of masculine ability; there still remains an enormous gallery of subsidiary portraits, for the most part faintly caricatured, of men and women who do stand for something in modern life; portraits that are valuable, interesting and memorable. Nevertheless, I submit that Mr Wells' novels will not live by reason of their characterisation.

The desire to write essays in this class of fiction does not seem to have overcome Wells until the last few years. Before 1909, he had written all his sociology and all his romances, with the exception of *The World Set Free*, but only three novels — namely, *The Wheels of Chance*, *Love and Mr Lewisham* and *Kipps*; and none of them gives any indication of the characteristic method of the later work.

The first of the three, published in 1896, is in one respect a splendid answer to the objection against what has been called the episodical novel. The story deals only with ten glorious days in the life of Hoopdriver, a callow assistant in a draper's "emporium" at Putney. He learnt to ride a bicycle, set out to tour the south coast for his short summer holiday and rode into romance. One section of the book is a trifle too hilarious, coming perilously near to farce, but underlying the steady humour of it all is a perfectly consistent, even saddening, criticism of the Hoopdriver type. He has imagination without ability; life is made bearable for him chiefly by the means of his poor little dreams and poses; he sees himself momentarily in the part of a detective, a journalist, a South African millionaire, any assumption to disguise the horrible reality of the draper's assistant; and yet there is fine stuff in him. (Perhaps the suggested antithesis is hardly justified!) We leave him at the door of the Putney shop full of resolution to read, to undertake his own education, in some way, no doubt, to better himself, as he might have phrased it. But we doubt the quality of his determination and of the lasting influence of the "more wonderful desires and ambitions replacing those discrepant dreams." We have only followed Hoopdriver through a ten-day episode, but all his story has been told.

We are in quite a different position with regard to Lewisham. The history of his encounter with love and the world, published in 1900, covers a period of four or five years, but while we leave him down-at-heel, with a wife and a mother-in-law dependent upon him, and the prospect of fatherhood adding to his responsibilities, we are uncertain whither his career will take him. Lewisham is the first sketch for the type that was to be elaborated in five subsequent books. The allurements of his love for Ethel Henderson spoilt his chances at the science school, but he has the quality that is so conspicuously lacking in the Hoopdriver-Kipps-Polly succession. Lewisham had some resolution, undoubted energy, and the beginnings of that larger vision which was the gift of the later protagonists. But he is not idealised; he comes nearer to the average of humanity than the later pictures of his like; although they share with him that tendency to sudden irascibility, to outbursts of a somewhat petty temper against the obvious limitations of life – a common tendency observable in nearly all Mr Wells' dominant male characters. Those few years of Lewisham's life were so well done, so consistently developed, that I have regretted the absence of a sequel. Indeed, I still regret it, although I realise very well that Mr Wells' steady progress in the conception of his own purpose as a writer has absolutely precluded any return to an older method. Lewisham was not

35

quite strong enough to portray the further development of the dominant idea, not a sufficiently tempered tool for the dissection of the modern world.

I have said little about the story of this fragment of Lewisham's career; I have not even mentioned that deliciously plausible and able rogue, Chaffery, the fraudulent medium; but in this essay I am more concerned to trace the meaning of Mr Wells' books than to criticise or praise the detail. With regard to the latter, the reader may always feel so perfectly safe. He need have no doubt that description of action, of mood, or of place will be vivid and convincing, true to life and essential to the story. I do not pass this detail by because I have found it better done in other contemporary writers; I have not; but because I find a pregnancy and a growing force behind these minutiæ that is strangely lacking from any other works of fiction in which I can find any comparison.

There are, however, still two more novels to be disposed of before I can examine the full expression of Mr Wells' purpose as I find it in his later books. One of these novels, *Kipps* (1905), is the next in chronological order; the other, *The History of Mr Polly*, was published in 1910, interpolated between *Ann Veronica* and *The New Machiavelli*. Both Kipps and Polly began active life in a draper's shop. The former is explicitly labelled "a simple soul." He is at once sillier and sharper than Hoopdriver, but, like that "dear fool" (the phrase is Mr Wells'), Kipps has some very sterling qualities. He had the good fortune to come into money — I cannot but count it good fortune in his case — and was just wise enough to avoid a marriage with Helen Walshingham — "County family. Related to the Earl of Beauprés" — and if he shirked that match rather from sheer funk than from any clear realisation of the futility of what he was avoiding, he did, at least, run away with and marry that very charming little house-maid, Ann Pornick, whom he had loved in his early boy-hood. After his marriage he lost the greater part of his money, and later recovered it again; but all these shocks of fortune left him the same simple soul, untroubled by any urgent problems outside the range of his personal experi-ence. His brief contact with the dreamer, Masterman, and his friendship with the capable young engineer-socialist, Sid Pornick, Ann's brother, only roused Kipps to a momentary wonder, and his final enunciation of the great question was representative. "I was thinking just what a Rum Go every-thing is," he says. That question, to quote Mr Wells, "never reached the surface of his mind, it never took to itself sub-stance or form; it looked up merely as the phantom of a face might look, out of deep waters, and sank again into nothing-ness."

Mr Polly is a third variant of the Hoopdriver-Kipps genus. He had more initiative, although he still presents a problem in inertia, and he is the only one of the three who had a feeling for literature, and read persistently, if vagari-ously. And Mr Polly did at last take his fate into his own hands, commit arson, desert his wife and wander off, an "exploratious adventurer," as he might have put it, to dis-cover some joy and poetry in life after a heroic battle that he funked most horribly and might have avoided. This may sound rather a criminal record, and even so I have taken no account of his fraud on the Life Assurance Company, but no one could ever condemn Mr Polly – or wish him a hap-pier employment than that he finally achieved partly by luck and partly by his own effort. He was the sport of the forces that break out so ungovernably in this haphazard world. As the "high-browed gentleman living at Highbury" explains: "Nothing can better demonstrate the collective dullness of our community, the crying need for a strenuous, intellectual renewal, than the consideration of that vast mass of useless, uncomfortable, under-educated, under-trained, and altogether pitiable people we contemplate when we use that inaccurate and misleading term, the Lower Middle Class. A great proportion of the lower middle class should properly be assigned to the unemployed and the unemployable." And that is the moral we may lay to heart from the presentation of these three quite lovable and quite futile draper's assistants. Their stories are told without didacticism; the method displays at its brightest Mr Wells' intimate knowledge and understanding of the life and speech of the class portrayed; the developments are natural and absorbing enough to hold the interest of the most idle reader; and here and there, perhaps, an intelligent man or woman may be stirred to realise that he or she is in part responsible for the futility of a Hoopdriver or a Kipps, or for the jovial crimes of Mr Polly. . . .

I come now to the six novels which represent most truly the striving, persistent idealism of the mature Wells. In these books he has come to the mastery of his own technique – so far as a man may ever master it. He admits that there remain inexpressible visions, he is apt at times to be overtaken by his own mannerisms (a fault that in no way affects the enjoyment or enlightenment of the average reader), but he has wrought and perfected a delicate instrument of style that is finely adapted to his purpose. I cannot avoid speaking of "purpose" in relation to these five books, and yet the word is misleading. I do not mean by it that Mr Wells has ever sat down to write a novel with the deliberate intention of converting an honest reader or so. But I do mean that he has tried very deliberately to express his own attitude in these books, and that whether or not he was intentionally a propagandist, he has done his utmost to explain and to glorify that attitude of his. Perhaps I shrink from that word "purpose" too sensitively, because it is so naturally associated in the mind with all that is clumsy and didactic in fiction. The "novel with a purpose," as the dreadful phrase has it, is a horrible thing, and none of this five could be so misdescribed. Nevertheless it is very plain that Mr Wells has deliberately selected his stories and his characters to illustrate certain points of view. The characters are consistent, and the story growing out of their influences and reactions is never distorted in order to score a point for the maintainer of a theory. But the preliminary selection cannot be overlooked. It has, without question, been made in each case to illustrate a thesis.

Ann Veronica (1909) opens an aspect of the sex question that has been amplified in later novels. The chief person in the story illustrates for us the revolt of young women against the limitations of a certain, the most representative, type of home discipline. Ann Veronica was a well-educated young woman with that leaning towards biological science which seems an almost necessary element in the make-up of Mr Wells' exemplars of the open mind. She came to an open quarrel with her father on the question of attending a somewhat Bohemian fancy-dress ball, and she had the courage and determination to uphold her declaration of independence. She ran away, came up to London from her father's suburb, took lodgings and essayed quite unsuccessfully to make her own living. She failed in this endeavour because she had not been educated or trained for any of those few and specialised occupations that women may attempt in modern conditions. She learned by experience various essentials that had been omitted from any teaching she had received at home, and ended that phase of her life by falling in love with Capes, demonstrator at the Westminster Imperial College, a man who was living apart from his wife. Ann Veronica's story is the first serious essay in feminism — a term that takes a much wider meaning in Mr Wells' definition than is commonly attributed to it. The novel presents the claim of the woman to free herself from the restrictions that once almost necessarily limited her sphere of action, restrictions that are ever becoming more meaningless in a civilisation that has enforced new economic conditions. But Mr Wells goes far beyond that elementary proposition. He has tried in *Ann Veronica* — and again with a more delicate probe in *Marriage* and *The Passionate Friends* — to touch the hidden thing that is causing all this surface inflammation. He has analysed and diagnosed the exposed evil, always it seems with a certain tentativeness, and we are left to carry on his line of research; many of the difficulties of the problem are indicated, but no sovereign specific for the malady.

Tono-Bungay (1909) touches only casually on the sex question. The involved love affairs of George Ponderevo are less essential than the career of his uncle, the inventor of the patent medicine that gives a title to the book. In many ways *Tono-Bungay* is the best novel that Mr Wells has given us. It is written in the first person, a narrative form that afterwards served to convey Mr Wells' interpolated criticisms of the bodies social and politic in something nearly approaching the shape of an essay, but in *Tono-Bungay* there are no important divagations from the development of the story. The framework of the book is provided by the life history of the narrator from early boyhood to middle age, matter interesting enough in itself even if it had not provided the means for revealing the inwardness of Edward Ponderevo's character and career. He was not a bad little man, this plump little chemist; a Lombroso or a Ferri would have found difficulty in classifying him as a "criminal type," however eager those investigators might have been to confirm their pet theories. Ponderevo's wife — the inimitable Aunt Susan — called him "Teddy" and his nephew endorses the appropriateness of that diminutive; he affirms that there was a characteristic "teddiness" about Uncle Ponderevo. He failed as a retail chemist in Wimblehurst. He was not naturally dishonest, but he had windy ideas about finance, and he was careless in the matter of certain trust monies. He was "imaginative, erratic, inconsistent, recklessly inexact," and his imagination led him by way of a patent medicine to company promoting on the Hooley scale. "Do you realise the madness of the world that sanctions such a thing?" asks Mr Wells in the person of the supposed narrator and points that question on a later page as follows: — "At the climax of his Boom, my uncle at the most sparing estimate must have possessed in substance and credit about two million pounds' worth of property to set off against his vague colossal liabilities, and from first to last he must have had a controlling influence in the direction of nearly thirty millions. This irrational muddle of a community in which we live gave him that, paid him at that rate for sitting in a room and scheming and telling it lies. For he created nothing, he invented nothing, he economised nothing. I cannot claim that a single one of the great businesses we organised added any real value to human life at all."

The enormous success and rapid failure of this futile, ambitious little chemist — a success that is, unhappily, only too conceivable and probable — are seen against the background of his nephew's life, Mr Wells has given a greater value and credulity to the legal criminalities of Ponderevo, by coming at him, as it were, through a wider angle; just as he achieves all the circumstances of reality in his romances by his postulation of an average eye-witness. But there are many threads in George Ponderevo's life that were not immediately intertwined with the *Tono-Bungay* career, and his love for Beatrice Normanby touches in quite another manner on the sex problem opened in *Ann Veronica*. In both these books the story is the essential thing, and the attack upon social conditions is relatively indirect. The general criticism is at times quite explicit, but it is subordinated.

In *The New Machiavelli* (1910) these relations are nearly reversed. The detailed exposure of the moving forces that stimulate our political energies, occupies long sections into which the human relations of Remington (the form is again that of an autobiography) hardly enter, except in an occasional conversation to sharpen up a criticism. This comment on politics (regarded in his own constituency, Remington says, not as a "great constructive process" but as a "kind of dog-fight") is the chief theme; subsidiary to it is the comment on a society that could waste so valuable a life as Remington's for the sake of a moral convention. Both comments point Mr Wells' expression of what he calls in this book "the essential antagonism . . . in all human affairs . . . between ideas and the established method — that is to say, between ideas and the rule of thumb." And he adds: "The world I hate is the rule-of-thumb world; the thing I and my kind exist for primarily is battle with that, to annoy it, disarrange it, reconstruct it." This confession is so lucid and characteristic that I cannot improve upon it, and yet I see that it is a statement likely to arouse considerable resentment, "Of course we are detestable," Remington admits in this connection; and in these later, more urgently critical novels, we recognise a little too clearly that note of protest, almost of defensive proclamation. And in none of them do we see it more definitely than in the book now under consideration. In many ways *The New Machiavelli* stands apart from the other novels. I find it a little bitter in places, because the thing condemned appears too small for such unequivocal condemnation. The following superlative summary is put into the mouth of a minor character, but I think it is fairly representative of Remington's later attitude. "But of all the damned things that ever were damned," says the plain-spoken Britten, "your damned shirking, temperate, sham-efficient, self-satisfied, respectable, make-believe, Fabian-spirited Young Liberal is the utterly damnedest." As a commentary, I find this exaggerated; and although it is in the mouth of one who is not presented as a spokesman for Mr Wells' own opinions, I feel that it comes very near to being a text for a considerable section of the political criticism; and that it indicates bias, a departure from normality.

And yet, despite this occasional exhibition of temper, *The New Machiavelli* is a most illuminating book. It reveals with extraordinary clearness the Wells of that period; but it also gives us a sight of the spirit in him that does not change. All his books, romances, novels and essays indicate a gradual process of growth; if we were to apply any label to him, we should inevitably land ourselves in confusion. He is nothing "in the first place" but a man with an intense desire to understand life. As he says in this book: "A human being who is a philosopher in the first place, a teacher in the first place, or a statesman in the first place, is thereby and inevitably — though he bring God-like gifts to the pretence — a quack." But while he may dissociate himself from any clique, and disclaim any fixed opinion that might earn for him the offensive and fiercely rejected label, he nevertheless presents to us one unchanging attitude in these very refusals. "I'm going to get experience for humanity out of all my talents — and bury nothing," says Remington; and that purpose is implicit in every book that Wells has written. He is an empiric, using first this test and then that to try the phenomena of life; publishing the detail of his experiment and noting certain deductions. But while he may offer a prescription for certain symptoms, he gives us to understand that he is only diagnosing a phase in human development; that he is seeking an ultimate which he never hopes to find, and that the deductions he draws today may be rejected tomorrow without a shadow of regret. He would be constant, I think, only in his inconstancy to any criterion of present conditions as applicable or likely to be applicable to the future; he sees life as a dynamic thing in process of change and growth. "All the history of mankind," he writes, "all the history of life has been and will be the story of something struggling out of the indiscriminated abyss, struggling to exist and prevail over and comprehend individual lives — an effect of insidious attraction, an idea of invincible appeal." And it is for this reason that he is so eager to battle with, annoy, disarrange and reconstruct that rule-of-thumb world he censures so steadily; he is fighting the assumption of a static condition which he knows to be impossible.

And for a moment in *The New Machiavelli*, and again in his next book, *Marriage*, he has a passing vision of some greater movement of which we are but the imperfect instruments. He develops and then drops the idea of a "hinterland," not only to the individual mind but to the general consciousness. The "permanent reality," he calls it, "which is never really immediate, which draws continually upon human experience and influences human action more and more, but which is itself never the actual player upon the stage. It is the unseen dramatist who never takes a call." And in another place he writes in the same connection: ". . . the ideas go on — as though we are all no more than little cells and corpuscles in some great brain beyond our understanding."

We come again to a hint of that explanation at the end of *Marriage*, published in 1912. The story, reduced to the barest outline, is that of the relations of Trafford to his wife. It is not complicated by any sexual temptations or jealousies, but it gradually evolves the integral problem of the meaning of life.

Trafford, before his engagement to Marjorie Pope, and for a year or two after his marriage, was engaged in research work. His speciality was molecular physics and he was a particularly brilliant investigator. That research, with all the possibilities that it held of some immense discovery of the laws that govern the constitution of inorganic and progressively, perhaps, of organic, matter, was sufficient to engross his mental energies, to give him a sense of satisfaction in life; but his six hundred pounds a year proved insufficient to satisfy the demands of Marjorie's claim to enjoyment. She was not a mere type of the worldly-minded woman. She represents, indeed, the claim of modern women for a distinctive interest and employment not less urgent and necessary than the interests and employments of men. And when she failed, as she plainly must have failed, to find any such occupation, her sense of beauty and her justifiable demand for life found an outlet largely in shopping, in entertaining, in all such ephemeral attractions and amusements as women in her class may seek and reject. That way of escape, however, soon raised financial obstructions to Trafford's work. He had to find a means for increasing his income, and came at last and inevitably to the necessity for making more money and continually still more. The road to wealth was opened for him and he took it by sacrificing his research work, but when the economic problem had been triumphantly solved, he could not return to his first absorption in the problems of molecular physics. Life pressed upon him at every moment of the day, he had been inveigled into a net.

The manner of Trafford's escape from the thing that intrigued him has been severely criticised. After I had first read the book I too was inclined to deprecate the device of taking Trafford and Marjorie into the loneliness of a Labrador winter, in order to set them right with themselves and give them a clearer vision of life. But I have read *Marriage* twice since I formed that premature judgment, and each time I have found a growing justification for what at first may seem a somewhat whimsical solution to the difficulties of an essentially social problem.

But in effect this is the same specific that I upheld in my comment on the romances; it illustrates the need felt by a certain class of mind for temporary withdrawal from all the immediate urgencies and calls of social life; the overwhelming desire to see the movements and intricacies of human initiative and reactions, from a momentarily detached standpoint. And Mr Wells has offered us a further commentary on the difficulties of this abstraction, by withholding any vision from Trafford until he was finally isolated from Marjorie, and even from any physical contact with the movement of what we call reality, by illness and fever. Only then, indeed, did he touch the vital issues. I find the statement of this ultimate thing, vaguely phrased in Trafford's semi-delirium, presenting another expression of the thought quoted from *The New Machiavelli*; the conception of humanity as an instrument. "Something trying to exist," he says, something "which isn't substance, doesn't belong to space or time, something stifled and enclosed, struggling to get through." And later he repeats: "It struggles to exist, becomes conscious, becomes now conscious of itself. That is where I come in as a part of it. Above the beast in me is that – the desire to know better, to know – beautifully, and to transmit my knowledge. That's all there is in life for me beyond food and shelter and tidying up. This Being – opening its eyes, listening, trying to comprehend. Every good thing in man is that – looking and making pictures, listening and making songs. . . . We began with bone-scratching. We're still – near it. I'm just a part of this begin-ning – mixed with other things. Every book, every art, every religion is that, the attempt to understand and express – mixed with other things."

I have reached something like a climax with this pas-sage; a climax that I would willingly maintain if it were possible, inasmuch as it holds a representation of that un-changing influence which I find as an inspiration and a force behind all H.G. Wells' books. Necessarily this vital inspiration is, as he says, "mixed with other things"; he has had to find a means to express it, and our means of expres-sion is limited not only by our own powers but in a large degree by the limitations of the audience addressed. More-over H.G. Wells' art represents him in that it is a practical art. He is, in an unspecialised sense, a pragmatist. He comes back from his isolations to find in this world all the sub-stance and potentialities of beauty both in outward appear-ance and in conduct. And he is not content to vapour of ideals. He recognises that the stuff of admiration and desire that animates his own being is present throughout hu-manity. Only the sight of it is obscured by all those stupidi-ties and condescensions to rule-of-thumb that he attacks so furiously. Those are the impediments that he would clear away, and he acknowledges that they stand between him and his own sight of beauty. He is compelled always to struggle – and we can see the signs of it in all he writes – with his own weakness and limitations; criticising himself as he satirises the thing condemned, but striving without ceasing to serve the purpose of that which he knows is "struggling to exist." This, to me, is the spirit of H.G. Wells, and I find it a spirit that is as admirable as it is human. . . .

The Passionate Friends (1913) is another experiment in exposition. The very real and fine love of Stafford (the auto-biographer in this case) and Lady Mary Christian is spoiled, made to appear insignificant and debased, by all the conventions and petty, unoriginal judgments that go to the making of the rule of our society. The woman had to make her choice between love in an undignified poverty for which all her training had unfitted her, and a sterile ease and magnificence that gave her those opportunities which her temperament and education demanded. She chose for dignity and opportunity, was tempted to grasp at love, and thus finally came into a blind alley from which death was the only escape. It is another picture of the old conflict illustrated in the persons of Ann Veronica and Marjorie Trafford; the constant inability that our conditions impose on the desire to love beautifully. The implicit demand is that for greater freedom for women, socially and economically. Incidentally we see that the man, Stafford, does not suffer in the same degree. His splendid love for Lady Mary is thwarted, but he finds an outlet. It is a new aspect of escape, by the way, for Stafford's illuminating business of spreading and collating knowledge is a relief from the scientific research which was in some form or another the specific of the earlier novels — if we exclude Remington's political propaganda in *The New Machiavelli*, a suggested solution that was, at the best, something half-hearted. And Stafford's escape, and his version of going to the mountain apart — by way of a sight of the East and of America — bring us back to that integral theme which

I have so insisted upon, even at the risk of tedious repetition. "I was already beginning to see the great problem of mankind," writes Stafford, "as indeed nothing other than a magnification of the little problem of myself, as a problem in escape from grooves, from preoccupations and suspicions, precautions and ancient angers. . . . For all of us, as for each of us, salvation is that. We have to get away from ourselves to a greater thing, to a giant's desire and an unending life, ours and yet not our own."

The last novel published at the time I write is *The Wife of Sir Isaac Harman* (1914). The same theme is presented, but in other circumstances. Ellen Sawbridge, when she married, at eighteen, the founder and proprietor of "The International Bread Shops," was an ingenuous schoolgirl; and for more than seven years the change from a relatively independent poverty to the luxuries she could enjoy as the wife of a man who had not outgrown the Eastern theory with regard to the position of women, sufficed to keep her reasonably content. Mr Brumley was the instrument of Fate that seriously disturbed her satisfaction; but she must have come to much the same crisis, if Mr Brumley had never existed. Brumley was a writer, but he was not one of "the really imaginative people, the people with vision, the people who let themselves go" — I quote the expression of George Wilkins, the novelist — and Lady Harman never fell very deeply in love with him. Nevertheless it was through Brumley's interference with her life that she faced the crux of her position as the closely restricted occupant of "a harem of one." She never broke out of that cage. One desperate effort led her, by way of a suffragist demonstration on a post office window, to a month's freedom in prison; but Sir Isaac and society were too clever and too strong for her. When she was enlarged from the solitude of confinement in a cell, she was tricked and bullied into the resumption of her marital engagements. And presumably she must have continued to act as the nurse of her now invalid husband for the rest of her life, suffering the indignities of his abuse and the restrictions of liberty that the paid attendant may escape by a change of situation, if release had not come through Sir Isaac's death. By that time Lady Harman had learnt her lesson. I am distinctly sorry for Mr Brumley, but I should have been seriously disappointed in Ellen Harman if she had consented to marry him.

Thus far I have only traced an imperfect outline of what I take to be the more important motive of the book. But there is a second pattern hardly less essential — namely, the criticism of the management and, à fortiori, of the conception of principle, in relation to the International Bread Shops. Arising out of this interwoven theme we come to some examination of the status of the female employee in general, and particularly in connection with the question of their board and lodging outside business hours. But in *The Wife of Sir Isaac Harman* the essay manner has been abandoned. Any diversion from the development of the story is carried out by the expressed opinions of the characters themselves; and, as a consequence, the two essential problems are not unduly intruded upon the reader, although for that very reason they may remain longer in his thoughts. One more comment should be added, which is that this is the wittiest book that Mr Wells has yet given us. However serious the motives that give it life, it must be classed as a comedy. . . .

In concluding this brief review of Mr Wells' novels, I feel that I must hark back to a passage in *The Passionate Friends* in order to indicate a spirit which, if it is not so definitely phrased in this last book of his, is certainly upheld in the matter of the story. For it is that spirit which seems to me the thing that should live and be remembered. Here is one of its more characteristic expressions in the mouth of Stafford, who writes:

"I know that a growing multitude of men and women outwear the ancient ways. The bloodstained organised jealousies of religious intolerance, the delusions of nationality and cult and race, that black hatred which simple people, and young people and common people cherish against all that is not in the likeness of themselves cease to be the undisputed ruling forces of our collective life. We want to emancipate our lives from this slavery and these stupidities, from dull hatreds and suspicions. . . . A spirit . . . arises and increases in human affairs, a spirit that demands freedom and gracious living as our inheritance too long deferred. . . ."

And surely H.G. Wells has striven to give a freer and more vital expression to that spirit, working through his own life, than any other novelist of our day. Indeed I would go further and claim that no such single and definite inspiration can be found in the works of any other secular writer. Wells has given to the novel a new criticism and, to a certain degree, a new form.

IV

SOCIOLOGY

Mr Wells' essays in sociology are not dry treatises, based on Blue books and the gathering together of information and statistics from a formless and largely worthless collection of earlier sources. He has approached this question of man in relation to the State in the same generous spirit displayed in his works of fiction; and it is only by using the word "sociology" in its fuller sense as conceived by Comte, rather than in the restricted sense of "social science" with its implication of economics, as narrowed by Herbert Spencer, that I dare to head this last chapter with so dangerously technicalised a term. Indeed, I would not use the word "sociology" now if I could find a more inclusive heading. For it must be obvious, I think, to anyone who has followed my exposition of the romances and the novels that Mr Wells has a way of treating all such subjects as relate to the betterment of humanity with a broad outlook, an entire disrespect for conventional forms however hallowed by precedent, and a habit of trenchant criticism that could hardly be fettered by an analysis of sociological literature or continual deference to this or that experiment in practice or theory. He approaches his subject with the normal mind of one who sees the world, its customs and rules of conduct, from what is, after all, the point of view of common-sense – another term that has been so grossly misused that the possessor of true common-sense is apt to be regarded as a most uncommon person. It is, in fact, the least common of qualities.

The first three books under this heading form some sort of a trilogy, and have a definite air of consequence. Of these, *Anticipations* was published in 1901, and *Mankind in the Making* and *A Modern Utopia* followed in 1903 and 1905 respectively. The scheme of the first two books combines a criticism of present conditions with a growing constructiveness that points the way to the ideal of what is called "The New Republic." Now, one of the labels that has been most frequently and adhesively affixed to Mr Wells is that of "Socialist," and no doubt it would proclaim his purpose admirably enough if we could satisfactorily define the word in its relation to him. But, personally, I refuse so to label him, because I know that socialism means as many things to different people as religion, and is as much a term of reproach in the mouth of some self-labelled individualists as the designation "Christian" might be in the mouth of the "true believers" — as the Mohammedans call themselves. Wherefore I am particularly anxious in approaching any description of "The New Republic," to make it quite clear that that idealised State is not built of the bricks that have been modelled and cast by any recognisable group of propagandists, working to permeate, or more forcibly to convert, a section of the public under the flags of, say, Fabianism or Social Democracy. The essential thing about Mr Wells is that he is not a Follower, whether of Marx, or Hyndman, or Shaw, or Bebel; he may have learnt from any or all of them, but his theory of social reconstruction is pre-eminently and characteristically his own. He does not believe in the private ownership of land, for example, but I do not remember that he has ever advocated the means of the "Single Tax." And in these sociological essays, as in his novels, his method is that of picturing the more desirable thing or condition, the method of sweet persuasion rather than that of the sectarian who has a pet specific. Nevertheless Mr Wells uses his sharpened weapon of satire with considerable effect when he contemplates and displays for us the world as he sees it today. I find no hint of sweetness or persuasiveness on that side.

It would be impossible in an exposition of this kind to dissect these essays in detail, nor would it be desirable. Many of the suggestions with regard to actual practice, suggestions that might be embodied in modern legislation, are open to criticism in detail, and I would not pin Mr Wells down to the letter of any one of them. He has certainly changed his mind on many points since he wrote these essays in constructive sociology, and the fact that he has so altered and enlarged his opinions is the best possible evidence of his reliability and sincerity. He is before all else devoted to the services of growth and progress. "To rebel against instinct," he writes, "to rebel against limitation, to evade, to trip up, and at last to close with and grapple and conquer the forces that dominate him, is the fundamental being of man." And no man can hope to dominate those forces, if he is content to let his opinions crystallise at the age of thirty-five or so. If he would retain his powers of criticism and construction he must have the patience and the energy to maintain the normal, receptive mind with which he is naturally endowed. Unfortunately with that endowment commonly comes another – namely, a tendency to avoid the irk or constant struggle by taking the line of least resistance; by adopting an opinion and upholding it in the face of all reason; and only a man of exceptional patience, courage and ability can keep himself free from the prejudices and fixed opinions which not only bring him a delusive peace and certainty but also are the means to worldly success.

So I would advise the readers of *Anticipations* and *Mankind in the Making* to be influenced by the spirit rather than by the letter of these two books. The spirit is definite enough; it is the spirit of humaneness, of a passionate criticism of all the evils, miseries and disease that are the outcome of our present haphazard civilisation; the spirit for a desire for order, wider prospects and opportunities, greater freedom for growth. Men are born unequal, with different tendencies, different desires, different potentialities, but there should be a place for every one of them in the great economy of "The New Republic." Each has to learn the lesson — for discipline is essential — that he is not an independent unit as regards his work, but a factor, more or less insignificant, in the sum of individuals that make up the greater State. The good New Republican "will seek perpetually to gauge his quality, he will watch to see himself the master of his habits and of his powers; he will take his brain, blood, body and lineage as a trust to be administered for the world."

Such, I think, is the spirit, the permanent principle of these two books. That remains and increases. The conception of the process by which the New Republic shall be built is less constant, and Mr Wells will change his opinions concerning it for just so long as he continues to grow. Should he ever adopt an inalterable policy, subscribe to some "ism," and wear a label, he would brand himself truly as inconsistent. Then, indeed, he would have contradicted himself. We search for truth never hoping to find it complete and whole; and he who is contented with a part denies God. . . .

A Modern Utopia (1905) is an attempt to picture "The New Republic" in being; a very different dream of reconstruction from that displayed in Edward Bellamy's *Looking Backward*, and *Equality*, but having nevertheless certain points of likeness to the former at least, and especially in the method of marking contrasts by a form of parallelism, by keeping the world as we know it within the circle of attention in order to break the paralysing illusion that we are moving in romantic and quite impossible surroundings. Mr Wells' machinery is slightly complicated. He takes two figures from the beginning of this twentieth century. The Owner of the Voice ("you will go with him through curious and interesting experience. Yet, ever and again, you will find him back at the table, the manuscript in his hand . . .") and the "botanist," a foil and a stimulator to the other expositor. "The image of a cinematograph entertainment is the one to grasp," writes Mr Wells in his preliminary explanation. "There will be an effect of these two people going to and fro in front of the circle of a rather defective lantern, which sometimes jams and sometimes gets out of focus, but which does occasionally succeed in displaying on a screen a momentary moving picture of Utopian conditions."

I think Mr Wells tried very valiantly to avoid the all too obvious mistake made by other Utopian builders, both romantic and practical. He began, I feel sure, with the admirable intention of depicting the people of the early twentieth century in new conditions, changed only in so far as they were influenced by the presentation of finer ideals and by more beautiful circumstance. He even introduced a contemporary critic of Utopian conditions in the shape of the talkative person, "a conscious Ishmaelite in the world of wit, and in some subtly inexplicable way a most consummate ass." But once we begin to postulate our Utopian villains, the reader's thought is distracted from the contemplation of the heroic which is the cement that binds every stone in the visionary city. In order to change conditions it is necessary to change much in the present cast of human nature. In a fiction of Utopia there is no place for a Napoleon, a Rockefeller, or an ambition-swelled Imperialist. So Mr Wells is driven with various hesitations and resentments to assume that the interactions of cause and effect have indeed tended to produce a sweeter-tempered, more generous race of men and women; that the spirit which moves us now to seek a larger liberty and a greater tolerance has been encouraged and increased by the exercise of its own tendencies and the sight of its own triumphs; and that those who set their minds to the building gain an added grace in the labour. It is a perfectly fair and consistent assumption, but Mr Wells has been warned by his predecessors, from Robert Owen back to Plato and forward to Edward Bellamy, that the designs for Utopia have always been flawed by an altered conception of the humanity that walks within the city; and he has begun by trying to avoid a fallacy and ended by begging a question that he might very well have convincingly argued.

By many people *A Modern Utopia* is definitely labelled as the "Samurai" book. That conception of a natural aristocracy of spirit and ability did indeed return upon its creator in the form of an object lesson that filled him with a disgust for what was really a fine ideal, only too temptingly displayed. So many of his readers, and particularly his younger readers, formed the wish to become "Samurai" without more ado, a high office for which none of them, perhaps, had the ability or the determination to fill. For Utopias take even longer to build than Rome or London. But the plan is there — vague and tentative as the original scheme of a Gothic cathedral, a plan to be continually modified and changed in its most important features; and the building has begun. . . .

The last books that can strictly fall into the present category are *The Future of America* (1906) and *New Worlds for Old* (1908). The former is rather a record of impressions than the attempt at prophecy which the title and the first chapter indicate; and the final conclusion is too hesitating even to convince us that America has a future. "I came to America questioning the certitudes of progress," Mr Wells says in his Envoy. "For a time I forgot my questionings, I sincerely believed, 'These people can do anything,' and, now I have it all in perspective, I have to confess that doubt has taken me again." And without question he has changed his opinion with regard to many of the observations he made nine years ago. I sincerely hope he has.

New Worlds for Old is quite definitely a book of suggestions with regard to certain aspects of socialism. It is the most practical of all the sociological books, and makes so strong an appeal to the buried common-sense of even prejudiced readers, that a devoted Primrose Leaguer to whom I lent my copy was quite seriously disturbed in mind for nearly a week after he had read it. Fortunately for his own peace, he found an answer that permitted him comfortably to avoid the perpetual burden of an active responsibility. He thought that "Socialism would be all right in a perfect world," or words to that effect; and it was quite evident to him that the effort to make some small contribution towards raising the standard of human idealism was no part of his duty. In any case he greatly preferred the solid assurance of the Primrose League. And, speaking generally, as I have tried to do throughout, I find that *New Worlds for Old* presents a clearer indication to the possible path for the idealist than any of the other sociological essays. *Mankind in the Making* dealt very largely with education directed to a particular end, but in the book I am now considering may be found certain outlets for the expression of the less consistently strenuous. Education, whether of individual children in the home or regarded as a function of the State, offers continual perplexities that only the most resolute can confront day by day with renewed zeal; the problems of collective ownership are less confused by psychology, and the broad principles may be adopted and the energy of the young believer directed towards the accomplishment of minor detail. He may, for example, find good reason for the nationalising of the milk supply without committing himself to any broader theory of expropriation.

Finally I come to the collection of various papers issued in 1914 under the title *An Englishman Looks at the World* – a book that I may pass with the comment that it exhibits Mr Wells in his more captious moods, deliberately more captious in some instances, no doubt, inasmuch as the various papers were written for serial publication – and that *Confession of Faith and Rule of Life*, published in 1907 as *First and Last Things*. The opening is unnecessarily complicated by the exposition of a metaphysic that is quite uncharacteristic and has little to do with the personal exposition that follows; and, indeed, I feel with regard to the whole work that it attempts to define the indefinable. I deprecate the note of finality implied in the title. "It is as it stands now," I read in the Introduction, "the frank confession of what one man of the early Twentieth Century has found in life and himself," but that man has found much since then, and will continue to find much as he grows continually richer in experience. So that while no student of Wells' writings can afford to overlook *First and Last Things*, I would warn him against the danger of concluding that in that book he will find at last the ultimate expression of character and belief, set out in the form of a categorical creed. Again I find a spirit and overlook the letter. I choose to take as representative such a passage as the following, with all its splendid vagueness and lack of dogma, rather than a definite expression of belief that Mr Wells does not believe in a personal immortality.

This passage runs: "It seems to me that the whole living creation may be regarded as walking in its sleep, as walking in the sleep of individualised illusion, and that now out of it all rises man, beginning to perceive his larger self, his universal brotherhood, and a collective synthetic purpose to increase Power and realise Beauty. . . ."

And now that I have attempted my interpretation, I look back and confess that it is a very personal reading of my subject. I may have sought too eagerly for all those passages in which I found a note that roused in me the most thrilling response. I may have omitted to display vital issues that more truly characterise H.G. Wells than the appealing urgencies, idealisms, and fluencies that I have found most sympathetic and most admirable. But if I appear to have done him an injustice in some particulars, it is rather because I have been absorbed by the issue I sought to reveal, than because I deliberately weighed and rejected others. This short essay can be no more than an introduction to the works it describes. It was never intended to be critical. I have had no intention of discussing technique, nor of weighing Mr Wells against his contemporaries in any literary scale. But I have attempted to interpret the spirit and the message that I have found in his books; and I have made the essay in the hope that any reader who may consequently be stirred to read or to re-read Wells will do so with a mind prepared to look below the surface expression.

I feel no shade of hesitation when I say that H.G. Wells is a great writer. His fecundity, his mastery of language, his comprehension of character are gifts and abilities that certain of his contemporaries have in equal, or in some particulars in larger measure. But he alone has used his perfected art for a definite end. He has not been content to record his observations of the world as he has seen it, to elaborate this or that analysis of human motive, or to relate the history of a few selected lives. He has done all this, but he has done infinitely more by pointing the possible road of our endeavour. Through all his work moves the urgency of one who would create something more than a mere work of art to amuse the multitude or afford satisfaction to the critic. His chief achievement is that he has set up the ideal of a finer civilisation, of a more generous life than that in which we live; an ideal that, if it is still too high for us of this generation, will be appreciated and followed by the people of the future.

A BIBLIOGRAPHY OF H.G. WELLS' PRINCIPAL WRITINGS

Select Conversations with an Uncle (*Lane*). 1895.

The Time Machine – An Invention (*Heinemann*). 1895.

*The Stolen Bacillus and Other Stories (*Macmillan*). 1895.

The Wonderful Visit (*Dent*). 1895.

The Island of Dr Moreau (*Heinemann*). 1896.

The Wheels of Chance (*Dent*). 1896.

*The Plattner Story (*Macmillan*). 1897.

The Invisible Man (*MacMillan*). 1897.

The War of the Worlds (*Heinemann*). 1898.

When the Sleeper Wakes (*Nelson*). 1899. [Afterwards published (1911) in a revised and altered edition, as "The Sleeper Awakes."]

*Tales of Space and Time (*Macmillan*). 1899.

Love and Mr Lewisham (*Macmillan*). 1900.

Certain Personal Matters (*Unwin*). 1901.

Anticipations of the Reaction of Mechanical and Scientific Progress upon Human Life and Thought (*Chapman & Hall*). 1901.

The First Men in the Moon (*Macmillan*). 1901.

The Discovery of the Future (A Lecture given at the Royal Institute). 1902.

The Sea Lady – A Tissue of Moonshine. 1902.

Mankind in the Making (*Chapman & Hall*). 1903.

*Twelve Stories and a Dream (*Macmillan*). 1903.

The Food of the Gods and How it Came to Earth (*Macmillan*). 1904.

A Modern Utopia (*Nelson*). 1905.

Kipps — The Story of a Simple Soul (*Macmillan*). 1905.

In the Days of the Comet (*Macmillan*). 1906.

The Future in America — A Search after Realities (*Chapman & Hall*). 1906.

First and Last Things — A Confession of Faith and Rule of Life (*Constable*). 1907.

The Misery of Boots (Fabian Tract). 1907.

Socialism and Marriage (Fabian Tract). 1908.

New Worlds for Old (*Constable*). 1908.

The War in the Air (*Bell*). 1908.

Tono-Bungay (*Macmillan*). 1909.

Ann Veronica — A Modern Love Story (*Unwin*). 1909.

The History of Mr Polly (*Nelson*). 1910.

The New Machiavelli (*Lane*) 1910.

The Country of the Blind and Other Stories (*Nelson*). 1911.

Floor Games (A book about play for children) (*Palmer*). 1911.

Socialism and the Great State (A contribution by H.G. Wells. The book is written by fifteen authors) (*Harper*). 1911.

Marriage (*Macmillan*). 1912.

The Passionate Friends — A Novel (*Macmillan*). 1913.

Little Wars (A book about play for children) (*Palmer*). 1913.

An Englishman Looks at the World (*Cassell*). 1914.

The World Set Free — A Story of Mankind (*Macmillan*). 1914.

The volumes marked * are collections of short stories, the best of which were republished in *The Country of the Blind*, 1911.

NOTE. — Some of these volumes have been published under different titles in the U.S.A. (See *American Bibliography*.)

66

AMERICAN BIBLIOGRAPHY

Island of Dr Moreau (*Duffield*). 1896.

Invisible Man (*Harper*). 1898.

Thirty Strange Stories (*Harper*). 1898.

When the Sleeper Wakes [English title, "The Sleeper Awakes."] (*Harper*). 1899.

Anticipations (*Harper*). 1902.

Discovery of the Future (*Smithsonian Institute Washington*). 1903.

Discovery of the Future (*Huebsch*). 1913.

Food of the Gods and How it Came to Earth (*Scribners*). 1904.

Love and Mr Lewisham (*Stokes*). 1904.

Mankind in the Making (*Scribners*). 1904.

Modern Utopia (*Scribners*). 1905.

Twelve Stories and a Dream (*Scribners*). 1905.

Kipps (*Scribners*). 1905.

Future in America (*Harper*). 1906.

Time Machine—An Invention (*Holt & Company*). 1906.

In the Days of the Comet (*Century Company*). 1906.

First and Last Things (*Putnams*). 1908.

New Worlds for Old (*Macmillan Company*). 1908-13.

Socialism and the Family (*Ball Publishing Company, Boston, Massachusetts*). 1908.

This Misery of Boots (*Ball Publishing Company, Boston, Massachusetts*). 1908.

War in the Air (*Macmillan Company*). 1908.

War in the Air (*Grosset & Dunlap*). 1910.

Ann Veronica (*Harper*). 1909.

Select Conversations with an Uncle (*Saalfield Publishing Company, Akron, Ohio*). 1909.

Tono-Bungay (*Duffield*). 1909.

War of the Worlds (*Harper*). 1909.

History of Mr Polly (*Duffield*). 1910.

History of Mr Polly (*Grosset & Dunlap*). 1912.

New Machiavelli (*Duffield*). 1910.

Door in the Wall and Other Stories (*Mitchell Kennerley*). 1911.

Floor Games (*Small, Maynard & Company, Boston, Massachusetts*). 1912.

Socialism and the Great State (*Harper*). 1912. (See page 119.)

Marriage (*Duffield*). 1912.

Little Wars (*Small, Maynard & Company, Boston, Massachusetts*). 1913.

Passionate Friends (*Harper*). 1913.

Wheels of Chance–A Bicycling Idyll (*Macmillan Company*). 1913. Illustrated by F.A. Symington. [English title, "The Wheels of Chance: A Holiday Adventure."]

The Wonderful Visit (*E.P. Dutton & Company*). 1914.

Social Forces in England and America (*Harper*). 1914.

The World Set Free (*E.P. Dutton & Company*). 1914.

INDEX

www.ingramcontent.com/pod-product-compliance
Lightning Source LLC
Chambersburg PA
CBHW031526040426
42445CB00009B/421